WORDS OF
INSPIRATION ON
Love, Faith and Hope

Samuel Aigbe

Balboa Press books may be ordered through booksellers or by contacting:

Balboa Press
A Division of Hay House
1663 Liberty Drive
Bloomington, IN 47403
www.balboapress.com
1 (877) 407-4847

ISBN: 978-1-5043-9014-9 (sc)
ISBN: 978-1-5043-9015-6 (e)

Library of Congress Control Number: 2017916055

Print information available on the last page.

Balboa Press rev. date: 10/24/2017

BALBOA.
PRESS
A DIVISION OF HAY HOUSE

Dedication

In loving memory of my mother Victoria Omenai Aigbe

Table of Contents

Introduction

According to St Paul, love, faith and hope are the three virtues that transcend time and are fundamental for our communing with God. These virtues are the reasons for our being and are the core foundations of our human relationships, as without them life will be void of meaning.

These poetic words of inspiration on love, faith and hope are intended as source of encouragement in our daily walk with God and in our relations with the people He brings across our path.

PART A
LOVE

Hope is the engine of the human spirit, faith is what keeps it alive and love is the oil that lubricates the human spirit.

Love is the oxygen the human hearts need for the
perfect functioning of the human spirit.

Love is the life-blood of the human spirit by which God
continually breathes His life into our being.

In Christ-like love, we not only love our enemies but also pray for them - for God's grace for healing and reconciliation.

In love we come to the completeness of ourselves; God's Spirit living in and through us, giving meaning to our lives.

Love is the light that shines brightly and never
goes dim reigniting broken hearts.

When we walk in love; God not only walks with us, He works through us.

Love is the medicine for unnecessary grief and pain.

We see the goodness of God in others by attending to their needs.

To see God in others is to love them unconditionally.

Once we have love for God, loving others becomes second nature to us.

To walk with God, we must first learn to walk in love.

Our love for God is demonstrated with the dignity
in which we respond to the needs of others.

The closer we are in acts of love and unity, the more real
God's presence becomes manifest in our lives.

We cannot say we love God and not have a relationship with Him, to love God is to have a relationship with Him.

We are all celebrants of God's love, Jesus is the reason
for the celebration, are you celebrating Him?

One of the most effective prayers we can pray is for the grace to be loving as Jesus loves us and forgiving as God forgives us.

God we pray for your grace to be loving as Jesus
loves us and forgiving as you forgive us.

Our fulfilment as humans is when we abide in
God's love and His love abides in us.

Our best expression of our love for God is through prayer; let us create time to pray.

God, we pray for Your continual grace for the renewing of our hearts and minds with deeper understanding to learn the lessons of Your love for us.

CONTRIBUTE

God give us the grace to see through the eyes of Your love for us.

forgive

God's love is meteoric,
His loyalty astronomic,
His purpose titanic,
His verdicts oceanic,
Yet in His largeness
Nothing gets lost
Psalm 36 : 5-6 MSG

God is love, to live in love, forgive yourself of your past
mistakes and the wrongs of others towards you.

Our little acts of kindness make a big difference in the
lives of those we affect with our kind deeds.

Let us live in love, love drives out all fear.

When we open ourselves to receive from God, we should be open
to share that we have received with those less fortunate.

The essence of our Christian faith is not just talking the talk but also walking the walk of forgiveness and love.

CONTRIBUTE

Our greatness as a person is on how we have impacted the lives of others with deeds of love and kindness.

When we respond in generous ways to the needs of others,
God reaches out to our needs in a more generous manner.

Our good intentions towards others anchor prosperity for us.

Love is the joy that overflows when we learn to accept our differences as humans.

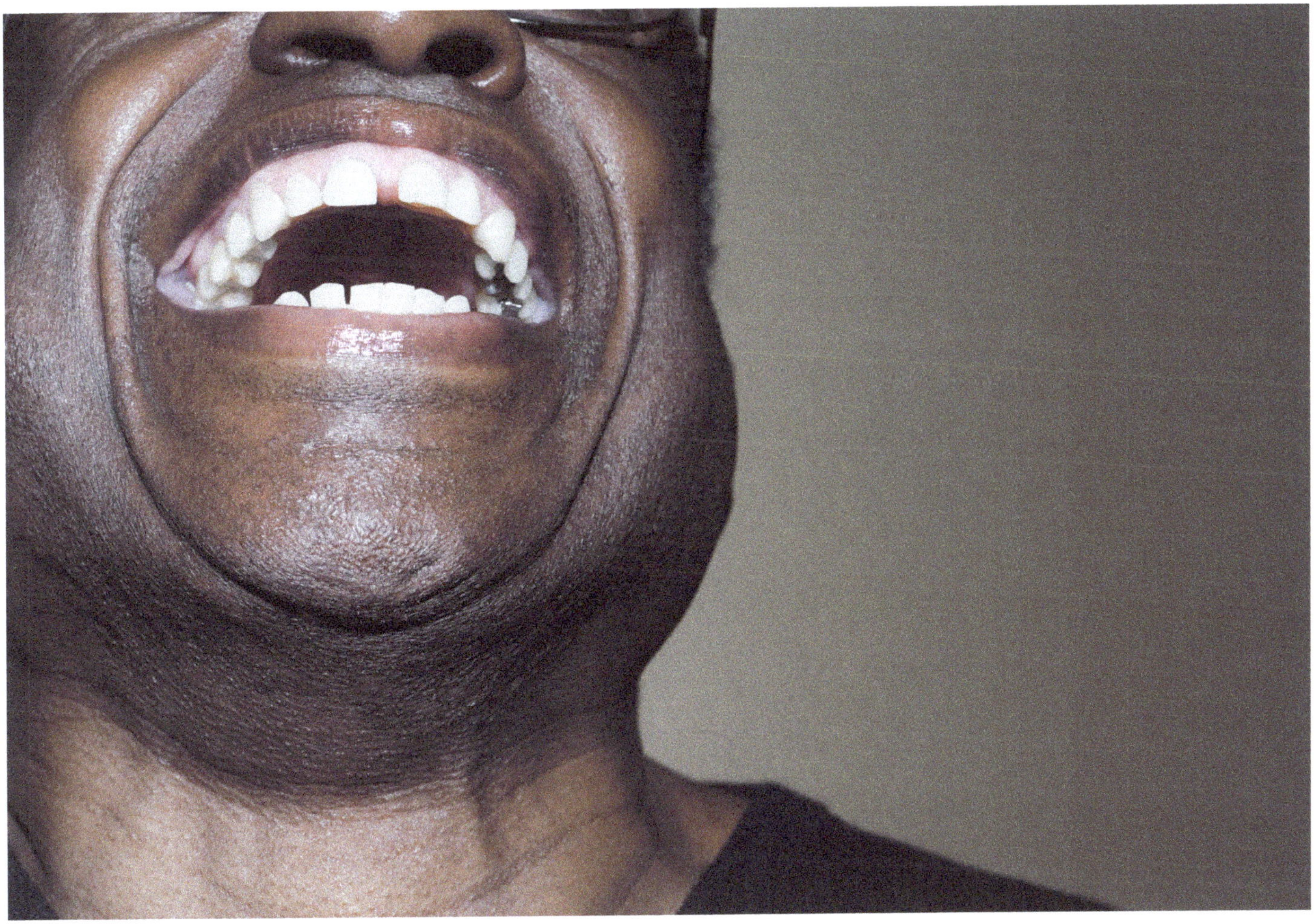

Forgiveness of the wrongs we have suffered in the hands of others opens us to the treasures of God: joy, peace and love.

Love and respect entails us not to make a snap judgement on the weaknesses of others but to build on their strengths.

The relevancy of Christianity depends on our willingness to be
a channel by which God's love flows through to others.

As tripartite beings we are engineered by God to be forming relationship centred on love: givers and receivers of God's grace.

73

Our human actions are only justifiable when is on
the absolute truth and brings about unity.

When we make others irrelevant to make
ourselves relevant, this makes us evil.

In the fluidity of life: the only thing that guarantees our survival is the realization for our shared humanity and our love for each other.

We 'Christians' have the responsibility of making
our pathways safe for others to tread.

We negate the requirement and forfeit the provisions of the Lord's Prayer if we fail to forgive those who have wronged us.

forgive

Before you commit an act or omit, ask yourself would your action or inaction not only benefit you, but also be of good to others.

In Christ-like love, we neither judge nor condemn others but through our words and actions we lead them to the embodiment of love 'Jesus'.

Men preach about religion, God talks about our relationship
with Him and the people He brings across our path.

Overcome evil with love, by so doing you help
bring the person from darkness into light.

Experiencing and sharing the love of God is the duty call
of all, particularly for every believing Christian.

The Bible narrative of the life of Jesus urges Christians to have faith and hope in God, love and forgiveness in our relationships with others.

Unforgiveness does to your spirit what the emptying of your litter or bin does to your dwelling. If you don't empty it, it makes for an unpleasant habitation.

To be willing to lose everything for the love of another is to gain everything.

Religion blinds us to the love of God, but true relationship and a walk with Jesus opens us to the grace of God, through the enabling and sustaining power of the Holy Spirit.

God is love; Jesus Christ lived out God's love for us when He died for our sins, His love is there for all to experience.

For every follower of Jesus Christ, God has enabled us with His Spirit of power, love and sound mind (self discipline).

Fruit of the Spirit worth cultivating: love, joy, peace, patience, kindness, goodness, faithfulness, gentleness, and self-control.

God's faithfulness is afresh, His mercies unbounded. His love is refreshing.

PART B
FAITH

To have God's confidence in us, we must learn
to cultivate faith in His leading.

With Jesus by your side, when you think you are losing, you are winning.

Our victory prayer, like Jesus, should be for God's will to be done in our lives; for God causes everything in the end to work for our good.

When it seems impossible, what you simply need to do is to say: Lord, I do believe. Help my unbelief.

Whatever challenges you are facing; God has allowed it, because
He's already determined the outcome for your good.

The manifestation of the supernatural (the virgin with a child) is the reality of the existence of a supernatural God.

Our dependency on God is not a weakness but our
strength in Him who is all powerful.

When we are down to nothing, God is up to something.

Grace makes the impossible possible. God only requires
from us faith the size of a mustard seed.

Logic and rationalisation deny us of God's grace,
but faith brings His love alive in us.

The act of receiving is reciprocated by a corresponding action of giving. What are we giving to God to enlarge our capacity to receive from Him?

God help us to be alert and watchful and not be complacent
in thinking that we have it all figured out.

From Jesus' life we are reminded that in our darkest moment that is when God is nearest to us, carrying us in His hands.

Faith questions not how, but gives us complete trust
and confidence in the promises of God.

Humility is God meeting us in our emptiness and
empowering us with His Spirit for greatness.

The baptism of repentance simply means we die to live and we live to die no more, because Jesus has paid the price for our sins.

When we diligently seek, follow and serve
God; He openly acknowledges us.

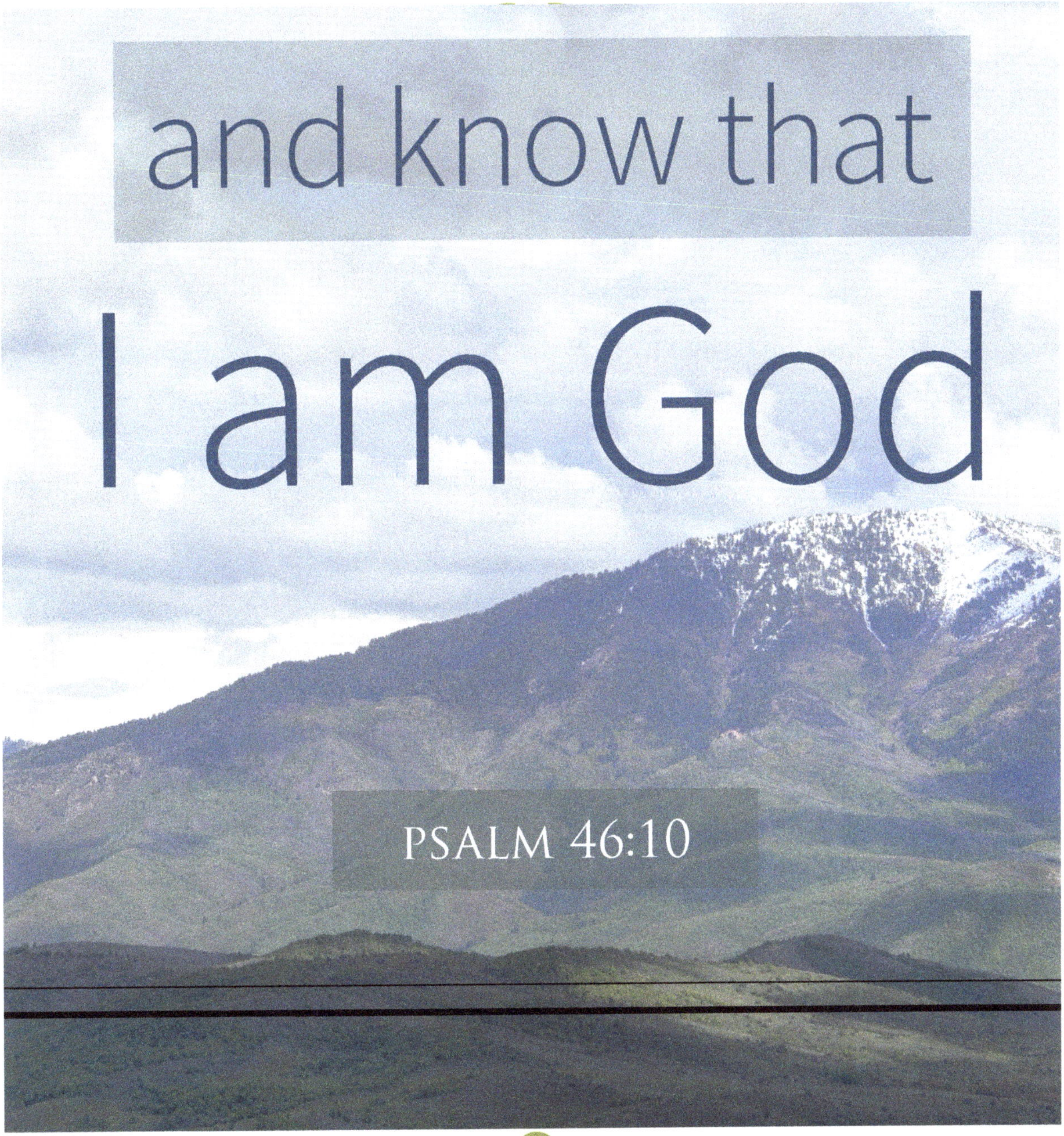

and know that

I am God

PSALM 46:10

Those who live in the shelter of the Most High will find rest in the shadow of the Almighty. Psalm 91:1

Teach me to do your will, for you are my God; may your gracious Spirit lead me forward on a firm footing.

Psalm 143:10 NLT

We find meaning in our lives in the purposes of God
expressed in His words — The Holy Bible.

A House is built by wisdom and becomes strong through good sense.
Proverbs 24:3

PART C
HOPE

Let our service be characterised by genuine love in serving You God, firm faith in the promises of Your Word and the hope of eternal life.

When self-pity and resentment set in, let us counter such negative emotions with a thankful heart.

When life seems challenging, replay your memories of past achievements. God has allowed the challenge for your next achievement.

Be thankful for who you are, the person you are admiring
is probably wishing to have the heavy cross he or she
is carrying exchanged for your light cross.

Trials and temptation are meant to refine our characters
and refocus us towards our God given goals.

God always give succour to the weak, when face with a Goliath like David acknowledges Him as the source of your strength.

The LORD is my Shepherd; I have all that I need.
Psalm 23:1 NLT

169

When tempted to grudge, let us be thankful for the many things we enjoy and often take for granted: health; family; friends and freedom.

God has given us a voice: to speak justly and fairly of others.

Joy is the contentment of the human spirit in the abundance of our wealth or in the circumstance of overcoming our poverty.

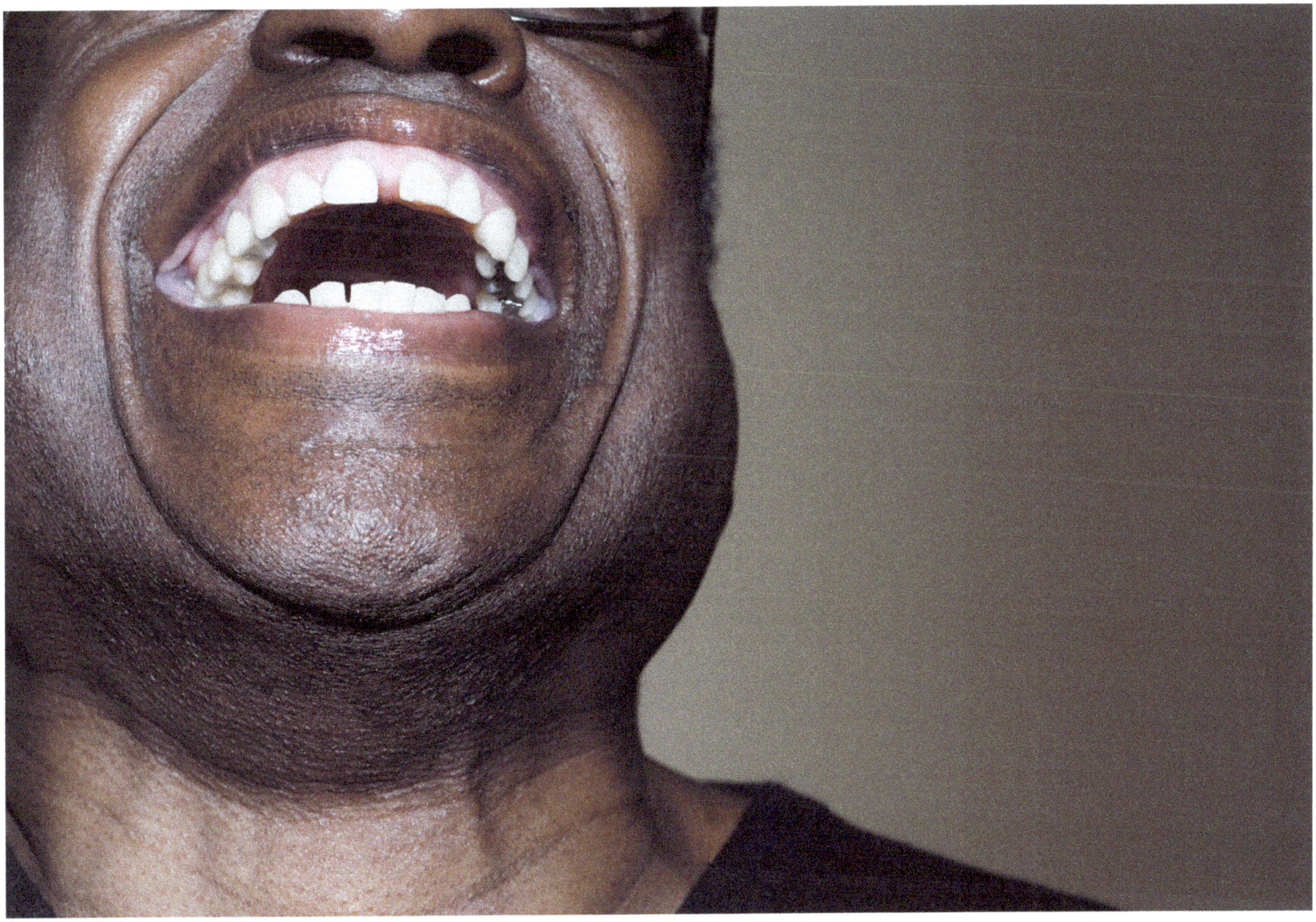

Grace is the presence of God in all His essence.

The ifs and buts of the past are the obstacles to our present opportunities.

Fear is the antithesis of our supposed failings.

The past is the mirror for the present, the
present the reflection for the future.

Guilt of our past mistakes imprisons the human spirit; the past is behind us, learn to forgive yourself and live in the freedom of the present.

All times and seasons are in the hands of God.
Only the wise know the use of it.

Labelling or generation robs us of our individuality, is best to get to know someone to gain an understanding of what makes him or her unique as an individual.

189

We live in regrets when we fail to learn the lessons of our failures; such missed opportunities must be seen as an avenue for our growth.

If all we do when we come to God in prayers is talkative, then we miss the essential of our communication with Him, which is listening.

God has given us all a platform - talent, gift, ability and position of influence; we are called to be the salt of the earth and the light of the world.

Our experiences - good or bad and the response we attach to it explain why we applaud certain character traits and despise others.

The mastery of an art or trade comes from repeated failures and the desire to exceed your expectations.

Life is a theatre; we all at the same time and in different stages play an active or inactive role.

When temptations assail us, God help us like Jesus
to be wise not to put you to the test.

Thank you Jesus for making Your Word alive in us
by the indwelling of Your Holy Spirit.

Instead of our usual want and need demands, let us spend more time in praising and worshiping God. Acknowledging Him for who He is.

With God nothing is impossible, because He has made everything possible in Jesus. Through Him we can do all things.

Our walk of faith is our affirmation of the omnipotence of God.

About the Author

Samuel Aigbe was one of ten survivors of the Kenya Airways flight KQ431 plane crash off the coast of Abidjan, Ivory Coast, on 30th January 2000, of which there were 169 fatalities. He holds a Bachelor of Science degree in Political Science and Public Administration from the University of Benin, Edo State, Nigeria.

In the aftermath of the plane crash, he gained two postgraduate degrees: Master of Arts in Human Rights, Ethics and International Relations; and Master of Law in International Law with International Relations both from the University of Kent, Canterbury, England.

In his previous book – 'A Plane Crash Survivor's Miraculous True Story', Samuel Aigbe told the incidents prior, during and after the plane crash. He shared his life as a testament of the goodness of God that saw him through that gruesome moment in the Atlantic Ocean.

ALSO BY SAMUEL AIGBE

A Plane Crash Survivor's Miraculous True Story

CPSIA information can be obtained
at www.ICGtesting.com
Printed in the USA
BVHW02s2352040718
520791BV00004B/8/P

9 781504 390149